my many emotions

Surprise

Published in the United States of America by Cherry Lake Publishing Group
Ann Arbor, Michigan
www.cherrylakepublishing.com

Reading Adviser: Beth Walker Gambro, MS, Ed., Reading Consultant, Yorkville, IL
Emily Fragapane, M.Ed., Ed.S., Nationally Certified School Psychologist, RYT200
Book Designer: Jennifer Wahi
Illustrator: Jeff Bane

Photo Credits: © Anatoliy Karlyuk/Shutterstock.com, 5; © Krakenimages.com/Shutterstock.com, 7, 11; © Oksana Kuzmina/Shutterstock.com, 9; © Syda Productions/Shutterstock.com, 13; © LightField Studios/Shutterstock.com, 15; © Monkey Business Images/Shutterstock.com, 17; © Prostock-studio/Shutterstock.com, 19; © Olena Yakobchuk/Shutterstock.com, 21; © Littlekidmoment/Shutterstock.com, 23; Cover, 2-3, 6, 14, 22, 24, Jeff Bane

Cherry Lake Press is an imprint of Cherry Lake Publishing Group.

Library of Congress Cataloging-in-Publication Data

Names: Devera, Czeena, author. | Bane, Jeff, 1957- illustrator.
Title: Surprise / by Czeena Devera ; illustrated by Jeff Bane.
Description: Ann Arbor, Michigan : Cherry Lake Publishing, [2021] | Series: My many emotions | Includes index. | Audience: Grades K-1
Identifiers: LCCN 2021004941 (print) | LCCN 2021004942 (ebook) | ISBN 9781534186972 (hardcover) | ISBN 9781534188372 (paperback) | ISBN 9781534189775 (pdf) | ISBN 9781534191174 (ebook)
Subjects: LCSH: Surprise--Juvenile literature. | Emotional intelligence--Juvenile literature. | Social learning--Juvenile literature.
Classification: LCC BF575.S8 D45 2021 (print) | LCC BF575.S8 (ebook) | DDC 152.4--dc23
LC record available at https://lccn.loc.gov/2021004941
LC ebook record available at https://lccn.loc.gov/2021004942

Printed in the United States of America
Corporate Graphics

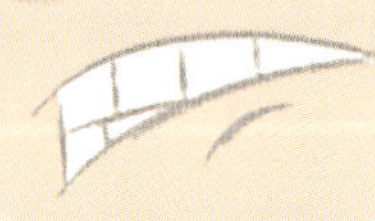

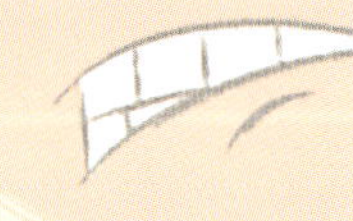

table of contents

About the author: Czeena Devera grew up in the red-hot heat of Arizona surrounded by books. Her childhood bedroom had built-in bookshelves that were always full. She now lives in Michigan with an even bigger library of books.

About the illustrator: Jeff Bane and his two business partners own a studio along the American River in Folsom, California, home of the 1849 Gold Rush. When Jeff's not sketching or illustrating for clients, he's either swimming or kayaking in the river to relax.

Have you ever heard a balloon pop? Did it feel like your heart stopped? That feeling is called **Surprise**.

Surprise comes **unexpectedly**. It only lasts a second.

Surprise can come with good things. A friend might visit a day early. A special gift could be waiting for you.

HAPPY

Surprise can also come with **unpleasant** things. A loud noise can make you jump. A friend could pop up and scare you.

Surprise can show up at any moment. Uh-oh, did your teacher call your name? Were you **daydreaming**?

How does Surprise feel to you?

Surprise might make you feel frozen in place. You might yell. You might feel your stomach drop.

These are all normal **reactions**. Your body is trying to figure out if you are in danger or not.

Surprise might feel scary at first. Take a deep breath. It’s good to take time to **recognize** how you feel.

Surprise can bring along other emotions. Like Happiness or even Sadness.

How do you show Surprise?

Remember, it’s okay to feel Surprise. It doesn’t last very long.

glossary & index

glossary

daydreaming (DAY-dreem-ing) to not pay attention, to dream while awake

reactions (ree-AK-shuhns) behaviors or attitudes in response to something

recognize (REK-uhg-nize) to understand and acknowledge

surprise (sur-PRIZE) the feeling caused by something unexpected or unusual

unexpectedly (uhn-ek-SPEK-tihd-lee) not expected

unpleasant (uhn-PLEZ-uhnt) not good

index